For my son, Kaden –

Through the clouds, across the stars, around the moon and back.

Love Mummy

Published by Peacock Press Australia 2018
www.peacockpressaustralia.com.au

Copyright ©Peacock Press Australia 2018
Meditation copyright ©Peacock Press Australia 2018
and produced by John St John

All rights reserved.

No part of this publication or meditation, both script and soundtrack may be reproduced, stored in a retrieval system, or transmitted in any form or by any means, electronic, mechanical, photocopying, recording or otherwise, without the prior written permission of the publisher.

Printed in Australia

ISBN -13: 978-0-6484041-0-1 (soft cover)

ISBN -13: 978-0-6484041-2-5 (e-book)

ISBN -13: 978-0-6484041-1-8 (hard cover)

Finding Your Happy Voice

Story by Teniele Arnold   Illustration by Pauline Murphy

Some days it was hard being little.

Some days Kaden felt sad,
some days happy,
some days angry,
and some days he just didn't know what he was feeling.

He had a lot of what his mummy called *"EMOTIONS"*.

One morning, he stomped into the kitchen, and said "Good Morning" to his mummy in a VERY grumpy voice.

"Oh!" said Mummy, "Kaden, I think you've lost your happy voice!"

Kaden wondered where his happy voice had gone.

He imagined a big, hairy gorilla in the jungle singing away with *HIS* happy voice!

But there were no gorillas around,
so that couldn't be it.

Or, what if Bunny from his room had come to life?

Was Bunny planning a day hopping all around a meadow somewhere, humming away happily with *HIS* happy voice?

Kaden ran down the hallway to his room and swung open the door, ready to catch Bunny escaping with his happy voice.

BUT ...

Bunny was right in the middle of the bed and Kaden's happy voice was nowhere in sight.

Maybe a whale had created a big ocean in the bathtub, singing whale songs with *HIS* happy voice.

But when he slid into the bathroom there was no big blue bathtub ocean,

no singing whale,

and no happy voice.

So, down the hallway he strode, hunting for his happy voice.

Next stop: the fridge.

Kaden imagined the big fish
Mummy bought for dinner, slicing through the water.

Had it come to life and swallowed his happy voice?

He pulled open the fridge doors and there was the fish!

But no, NO happy voice.

All this imagining of wild animals and dinner coming to life was getting quite *EXCITING!*

Kaden barrelled through the house, rolled across the lounge room floor, and dove behind the couch.

He thought he'd spotted a *LION!*

Had the lion snapped up *HIS* happy voice, in his big jaws?
Was he using it to roar orders to other wild animals?

Kaden jumped out, but there were no wild animals,

and *HIS* happy voice was still missing.

Who else could have stolen his happy voice?

He suddenly realised the dogs were outside!

Perhaps they'd taken it so they could talk to each other in *HUMAN!*

Kaden scrambled outside and snuck up to listen to the dogs,

but Chilli and Lulu were BARKING!

Dog, and not human after all.

They did not have *HIS* happy voice.

Disappointed, he headed back inside and flopped down at the kitchen table in a huff.

He'd been feeling OK before his happy voice went missing, but now he was feeling a terrible mixture of frustrated and sad.

Where could *HIS* happy voice be?

"You look sad Kaden," said Mummy,
"Have you not found your happy voice yet?"

"Noooooooooo...", wailed Kaden,
" I've checked EVERYWHERE!"

"I've been through the jungle past hairy, singing gorillas, run along meadows, chasing humming bunnies, swimming in the ocean with song loving whales, across the plains with a bossy, roaring lion, and out in our backyard chasing the dogs.

But MY happy voice is nowhere.

I can't find it. I can't find my happy voice.

I think it's *LOST!*" he said, grumpily.

Mummy was chuckling by the time Kaden finished telling her about all his adventures. Kaden felt a bit confused.

Mummy gave him a hug and looked him in the eyes, smiling.

Kaden always felt better when his Mummy smiled at him.

"Your happy voice isn't lost!" said Mummy, "It's here."

And she pointed to his heart.

"Everyone has a happy voice deep inside.

"We can find it if we close our eyes and imagine a ball of light in any colour, surrounding our heart.

It's warm and keeps you safe.

I know you can do it because you have the best imagination of all."

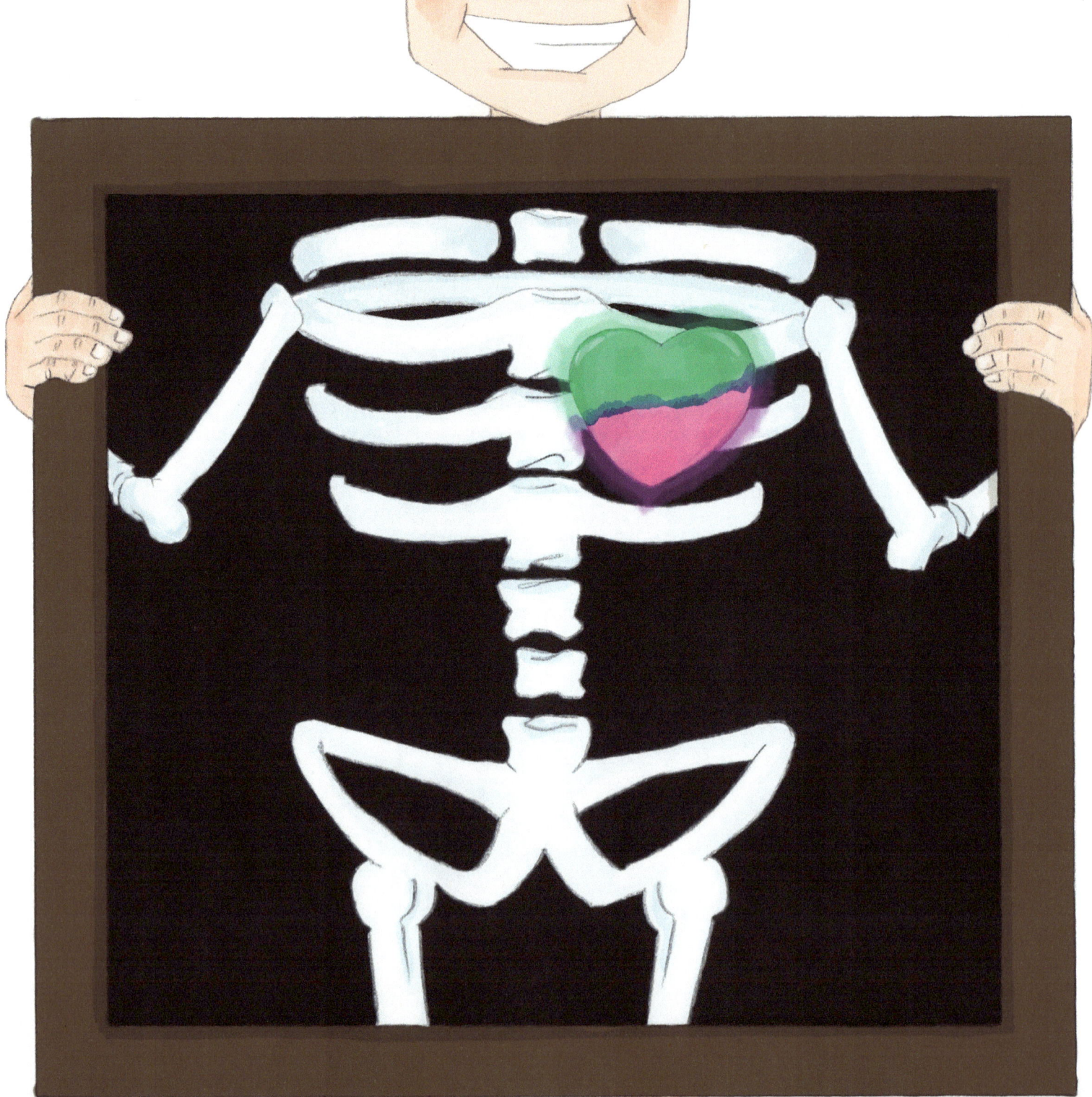

And suddenly, Kaden realised he did feel warm, safe and happy when he imagined the ball of light around his heart.

"This is where you can find your happy voice, and how you can *FEEL* it," said Mummy,

"*NOT* in the jungle with a hairy gorilla,
or in the ocean with a singing whale."

"Let's find your happy voice together."

"To find our happy voice we need to place our hands on our heart like this…"

Mummy took Kaden's hands and places them over his heart. "Take a big breath in and then a slow breath out, three times."

Kaden's Mummy held up three fingers.

Kaden and Mummy breathed in and out, listening to the sound of their breath and feeling all the feelings.

Kaden could hear the whale song, the ocean waves, and tall grass rustling on plains where lions sleep.

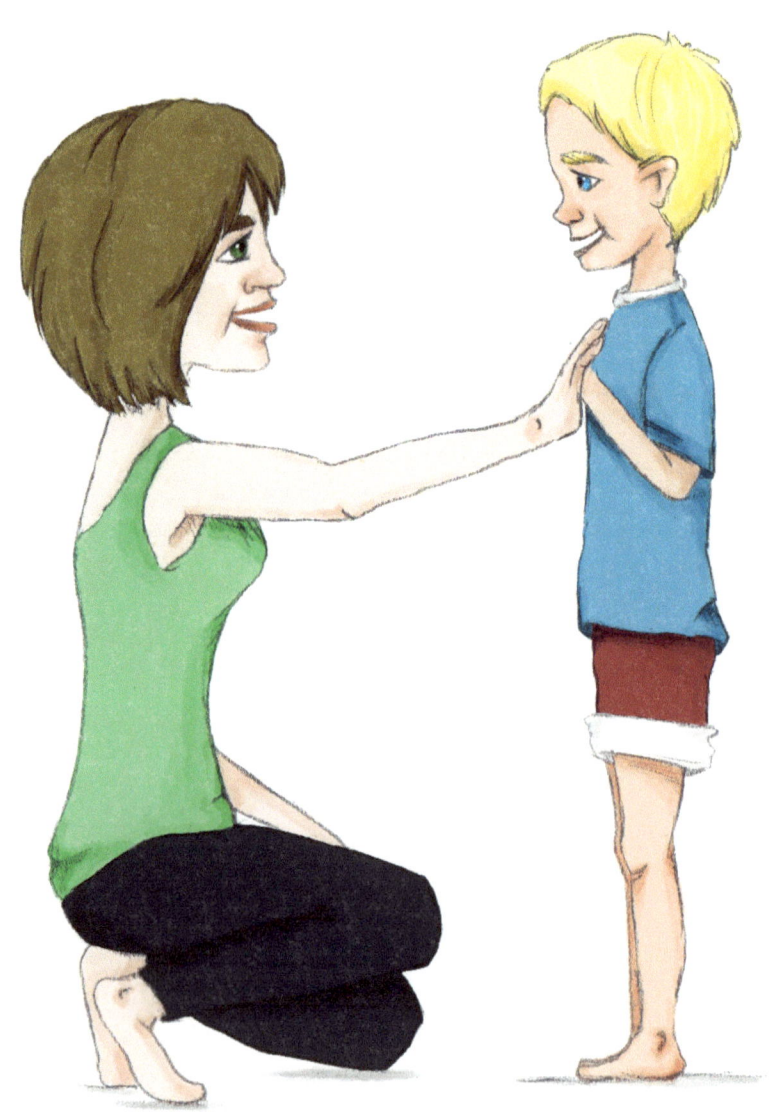

Then Mummy said, "Can you *FEEL* your happy voice?"
And Kaden could.

"Once you feel your warm, light energy ball around your heart, you can speak out with your happy voice."

"But what if I am sad?" Kaden asked his Mummy.

"Being sad is OK!" said Mummy,

"But if you try to find your happy voice, and speak with it, it will help me understand how you're feeling."

Kaden was just about as relieved as he had been the moment he'd realised there wasn't a lion in his lounge room.

Kaden practiced again -
he put his hands on his heart, took three deep breaths, felt the warmth around his heart,
and found his happy voice.

"Mummy, do you think the wild animals would have breakfast with us?" he asked.

Mummy laughed loudly and hugged Kaden tight.

"You never know, Kaden."

And although Kaden still liked the idea of a whale in the bathtub, he was pleased to know *HIS* happy voice was inside his own heart.

NOT in a jungle, *OR* an ocean.
NOT in a meadow,
and *NOT* with a lion.

He just needed someone who loved him
to help him understand how he could feel
HIS happy voice!
Right there in his own Heart.

A guide for parents

Just like so many other teachable moments, parents can add the story from 'Finding Your Happy Voice' to their parenting toolbox. Read this book together with your child/ren to help learn to recognise and connect with their feelings. Help your children come to their own inner stillness — to take a moment in a busy life, to pause and be present and listen to the voice inside — our inner happy voice.

When we become disconnected and unsure of how we feel, sometimes we lack the best way to communicate how we are feeling with the ones we love. This is no different for children.

We can all better communicate with the people in our lives when we understand how to truly feel our feelings and how to express them in a positive way, even if we are feeling angry, frustrated, or sad. We can still pause and express the feelings – without the negative attachments to the emotion — and then express ourselves in a more mindful way.

There is a free short meditation in this book. The longer version is downloadable from www.findingyourhappyvoice.com You can use this before bedtime as a nice story meditation, to wind down and relax before sleep. The short version in this book can be added into your daily practice as a parenting tool for those "in the moment times". It could be your little one is starting to look frustrated, or you can feel a tantrum coming on, or you yourself are having feelings of being overwhelmed by frustration or anger. You can use this quick meditation and breathing technique to help you to both communicate mindfully together, catching the moment before breaking point.

You could also give your child a special stone of their choosing to hold. Encourage them to imagine the stone's colour when they are doing their 'three breaths' breathing technique. You could try rose quartz or rainbow fluorite to represent the heart centre and perhaps allow them to keep the stone in their pocket so it's easily accessible. At first you may need to prompt them to use it, but after a while they will do it themselves any time they feel they need to find their happy voice, or need help to keep calm. They can place the stone on their heart and take three breaths. It's another way to connect with the energies of the stone and have a focus point, and to guide the breath into the present moment.

Finally, to you, my fellow parents and guardians. May your inner happy voice be constant, may your mindfullness come more easily, and may you enjoy every moment of guiding the young people in your life towards a present, joyful adulthood.

Finding Your HAPPY VOICE – Breathing Meditation

STOP
Get down low – Connect and place your hand on your heart

Breathe IN and OUT
3 times – Try to make mum and dad's eyelashes move!!

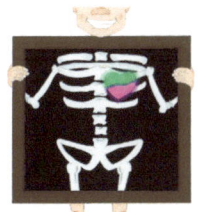

Notice how your body feels...
breathe in more if you need to

Tell mum or dad
– with a happy voice – how they can help you

Hug it out!!
Move through the day knowing you can find your happy voice at any time

Scan this QR Code to download your free full length Finding Your Happy Voice meditation.

ABOUT THE AUTHOR

Teniele Arnold is a free spirit, unafraid to fail while constantly striving to reach her dreams and goals. Her professional career includes photographer, author, and bookkeeper. She consciously blends her professional roles with yoga, reading, and being a loving parent of two strong-willed children – Elliana and Kaden – and a soul mate to Ashley. Teniele believes life is always going to have 'bumps', but when you bring yourself back to the moment and get clear on your own truth, anything can be overcome. Writing a children's book was a lifelong dream. Ensuring her book works to connect the readers and their families to forge together with presence, mindfulness, and find their inner 'happy voice' was an important part of the project. May you find 'your happy voices' and share them with your children.

– Teniele Arnold

ABOUT THE ILLUSTRATOR

Hello little sprites, my name is Pauline. I am a Mum of two superstar children, as well as an illustrator, graphic designer and animator based in Perth, Western Australia. I have worked in graphic design for twelve years and found my own happy voice in illustration! Finding Your Happy Voice is the first children's book I have illustrated. I would love for my work to help you find your happy voices too, just like Kaden!

– Pauline Murphy

ABOUT THE EDITOR

Jay Crisp Crow is a multi-award winning writer, presenter, and ex-showgirl who discovered her favourite role was the one she grew up thinking she'd never take on – that of 'Mummy'. She raises a hilarious almost adult, shining light of a teenager, and smart-as-a-whip 5-year-old in an 85-year-old cottage in Western Australia filled with children, creatures, friends, music, mess, and happy voices.

– Jay Crisp Crow

ABOUT THE YOGA & MEDITATION TEACHER

With our busy lifestyles and an array of constant stimulation, it is easy to be distracted and feel off balance. Learning to relax and calm the mind is something Jody Di Mascia has focused on and caught the attention of many, including her students of yoga, through her reassuring, calm and soothing voice. Through decades, with varying techniques of relaxation and meditation, she has continued to learn and share these benefits to bring you to a state of self-awareness and presence of mind.

– Jody Di Mascia

CPSIA information can be obtained
at www.ICGtesting.com
Printed in the USA
LVHW072002080720
660098LV00012B/573

Made in the USA
Columbia, SC
02 September 2022